CYBER SECURITY FOR KIDS

DR DHEERAJ MEHROTRA

Made with ♥ on the Notion Press Platform
www.notionpress.com

Contents

Preface

Understanding the work that will be done on the following techniques should be a top priority for all parents, teachers, and school leaders.

This is to provide further insight into the concerns about the same. It is more necessary; Kids should be educated about cyber security early because the skills they gain will help safeguard them as they age and experience more digital hazards. The main reason for this is because it is more required. I do not doubt that the book will serve as a manual for all parties investigating the concept.

Cheers, and best of luck with your studies!

Author

www.authordheerajmehrotra.com

CHAPTER ONE

What is Cyber Security?

"I really think that if we change our own approach and thinking about what we have available to us, that is what will unlock our ability to truly excel in security. It's a perspectives exercise. What would it look like if abundance were the reality and not resource constraint?"
— Greg York

Computers, servers, mobile devices, electronic systems, networks, and data are all vulnerable to hostile assaults. Protecting these things from the many forms of intrusions that might occur is called cyber security. Amongst other names, it is also known as electronic information security and information technology security. Another name for it is information system security.

It is of the utmost importance that you teach your kid the fundamentals of social engineering schemes like phishing and other security threats like ransomware and other viruses created to steal personal data or intellectual property. Because online dangers may arise at any moment and from any location, you must educate your youngster about the many cons that can be encountered online.

The phrase may be used in a broad number of settings, ranging from commercial computing to mobile computing, and it is simple to categorize it under a few of the most common titles in the industry.

“It takes 20 years to build a reputation and few minutes of cyber-incident to ruin it.” – Stephane Nappo

CHAPTER FOUR

Precautions

It is impossible to compare the amount of anonymity offered by the internet, and that of the actual world since the internet provides a far higher level of privacy. People can conceal their genuine identities and even carry on conversations as if they are talking to someone else entirely thanks to modern technology. Because of this, there is a chance that young children and teens who use the internet might end up in circumstances that are very dangerous for them.

Online predators who prey on children and teenagers may attempt to meet with their victims in person or engage them in the sexual discussion if they can gain their trust. Harassment may take the form of sexual predators sending explicit information to children's email addresses or requesting for pictures of the children to be transmitted to them. This is just one example of how this might happen. Because of this, it is of the utmost importance that you instruct your children to exercise caution whenever they use the internet since doing so may put them in contact with a material that might be potentially hazardous to their health.

- *Predators are more likely to target adolescents because of their age group. Even though they know the potential risks, they may engage in open conversation with a potential predator because they are eager to be accepted and satisfy their natural curiosity. This is because they have a great need to be accepted by society. Teenagers may erroneously believe that they have formed romantic emotions for someone they met online, which may increase the likelihood that they may agree to meet in person at some time in the future.*

- *Even though it is not necessarily probable that this will take place, there is still a potential that an adult who abuses children may establish contact with your kid. This is the case even if it is not necessarily likely to occur.*

This is referred to as the "contact risk," and the following are some recommendations you may urge your children to take to help keep them safe from bullies and other dangerous folks online. You will be able to get further information on the protection of your children while they are using the internet here.

• Refrain from using screen names or graphics that might be construed in a derogatory way at any time. These actions could attract the notice of those who prey on children online, which should be avoided at all costs.

• If you are given a compliment in a public forum online, you should note who gave it to you and express gratitude to that person. Even while there are a lot of highly decent individuals on the internet, there are also those predators who would attempt to build a connection with a young person by being overly charming. This is something that should be avoided at all costs. Even though this does not imply that you have to view every single person

with suspicion, you should practice extreme caution.

- *You shouldn't engage in any form of conversation with the other users in the chat who are trying to get too personal with you. You must end the discussion and prevent the other person from bringing up sensitive topics such as sexual or emotional worries if they are interested in doing so. If you permit yourself to engage in a discussion (or a relationship), it will likely be more difficult for you to remove yourself from the situation later.*

It is important to remember that individuals are not always who they claim to be; hence, it is preferable not to believe all they say. Keeping this in mind is necessary. Online predators who communicate with children could do so by pretending to be youngsters or teens so that they can have chats with the children. They may use a fictitious profile photo and add more content to their page to give the impression that they have higher credibility.

It is not a good idea to make plans to meet up with someone you have just spoken to online.

Therefore you shouldn't do it if you can help. Adults who prey on children or adolescents may attempt to set up a meeting with the victim in person at some time in the process. This might take place at any stage in the process. It would be best if you did not partake in this activity at any cost, regardless of whether the other person gives off the idea that they are friendly.

• *You must promptly inform a responsible adult with complete faith, such as a parent if you are in a precarious circumstance. Come across someone on the internet who makes you feel uncomfortable for whatever reason. You should immediately report that person to an adult responsible for you or a parent. In addition, you*

should make sure that you keep copies of all of your emails and other forms of contact if you need them as proof later. This might happen at any point in the future.

CHAPTER FIVE

Cyberbullying

A sort of bullying or harassment that takes place via the use of electronic means is referred to as cyberbullying or cyberharassment. Bullies don't need to be in the same room with the individuals they victimize to harass or intimidate them, just as sexual predators don't

need to leave their homes to have contact with minors. This holds for both face-to-face harassment and intimidation and that which occurs online. As a result, bullying behaviour, which bullies are notorious for, is becoming far less challenging. The unfortunate reality is that in today's world, bullying in any form, including cyberbullying that occurs via various social media platforms, is too widespread and does just as much damage as any other kind of abuse. This is a horrifying reality that has to be addressed.

This is a truth that has to be taken into consideration. You may help lower the risk that your children will be placed in dangerous situations by preventing them from creating social media accounts in the first place. This will help reduce the likelihood of your children being put in difficult situations. Because of this, you can shield them from any possible damage. Even though it is undoubtedly one of the most challenging obstacles to conquer, there is a solution to this issue that can be implemented, and it may be successful. Tell them that when they are older, they will be able to create their own based on their likes and preferences and that they will be able to do this independently with more experience.

could become the target of persistent harassment within the context of online gaming, thereby transforming the experience from one of creative inquiry into one of public humiliation that could lead to cyberbullying across some different online platforms as well as in real life.

- *Your comfort level when talking to your children about what is going on in their lives both online and in real life (IRL), as well as how to stand up to bullies, is the best foundation for protecting them from being subjected to cyberbullying. Talking to your children about what is going on in their lives online and real life (IRL), can also help them learn how to stand up to bullies. Your children may learn how to stand up for themselves against bullies by understanding what's going on in their lives, both online and in real life (IRL), and talking about it with their parents.*

There is no substitute for having a conversation with your child regularly, but using cybersecurity software and specialized tools that let you monitor your child's behaviour online and on their mobile device could be helpful. However, nothing can replace having a conversation with your child face-to-face.

CHAPTER SIX

The Safety Measures

The safeguards for the welfare of children and adolescents:

Children between the ages of 12 and 15 are more susceptible to being groomed or manipulated by adults they meet online. This is because children in this age range are more likely to have access to the internet. This is particularly true for youngsters in their preteen and teenage years.

Cyber-Security is much more than a matter of IT.Stephane Nappo

Young children do not yet have the cognitive capacity to understand the idea of social boundaries. They could post personally identifiable information (PII) online, such as on their social media accounts, that they shouldn't have made accessible to the general public in the first place. This might be a security risk. This might be anything, from images of humiliating personal circumstances to the locations of their houses or the plans for the trips their families go together.

The most effective form of protection is a solid Internet security package that can detect potentially harmful links and check every download for indicators of infection. This kind of package is the most effective form of defence because it is the most effective form of protection. For youngsters to effectively navigate the internet, it is incumbent upon them to have a firm grasp on responsible online behaviour and safety.

If we change our approach and think about what we have available, that will unlock our ability to excel in security truly. It's a perspectives exercise. What would it look like if abundance were the reality and not resource constraint?Greg York

Parents must instil in their children the habit of exercising extreme care whenever they are connected to the internet. This is because the internet is home to a vast number of websites that contain hazardous content. When using internet services such as social networking websites, gaming websites, and chat rooms, it is essential to practice extreme care at all times. If your children have mobile phones, they need to practice the utmost care anytime they are texting on their devices or accessing the internet on their devices. If they can do so, you can be confident that they will.

- *A significant portion of what your children post online could be accessible to the general public, but not the whole thing. This suggests that you can see it as well, and it won't do any harm if you tell them that if Mom and Dad can see it, then everyone else can as well since this is what the evidence suggests.*

"Even the bravest cyber defense will experience defeat when weaknesses are neglected."
— Stephane Nappo

You may decrease the possibility that they would participate in inappropriate online conduct by placing the computer in a communal place in the house where more people can view it. This will increase the number of people who can observe what they are doing on the computer.

Steer clear of spying on your children, but have open and honest dialogues with them about the consequences of public restrictions, both for your children on an individual level and for your family.

have access to many systems that might be used as targets for their attacks. If there is no memory Resident Program active on the host or client computer system, it will have a significant impact.

Because of the nature of breaches in electronic security, it is exceedingly difficult to apply current laws like breaking, destroying property, or stealing to such acts of criminal behaviour. Because of this, several nations have recently enacted new laws to combat what is now often referred to as "cybercrime." Regrettably, many of these rules are either too vague or demonstrate that lawmakers do not comprehensively understand the facets of computer hacking and security and the distinctions between electronic and physical surroundings.

An excellent illustration of this may be seen in the Digital Millennium Copyright Act passed in the United States. Although there are laws that can be used to deal with crimes committed online, it is equally as important, just as it is in the real world, to take appropriate precautions to protect oneself. These include choosing passwords that are difficult to guess, safeguarding sensitive data with encryption, and putting up a firewall.

In several nations, citizens get significant financial compensation for reporting to higher levels of government the use of unlicensed or pirated software; in these nations, the users of such software are subject to monetary penalties equal to double the cost of the product.

In digital era, privacy must be a priority. Is it just me, or is secret blanket surveillance obscenely outrageous?Al Gore

EMAIL ETIQUETTE

When communicating with others on the Internet, you will often use email as your first point of contact, and it may even be your sole point of contact. Even though everyone has their unique writing style, here are a few basic guidelines about behaving appropriately while communicating by email.

1. Avoid using too many quotes.
2. Maintain the privacy of e-mail communications.
3. Don't jumble up people's names.
4. Do not send out messages to everyone without regard for their specific interests.
5. Give it some thought before you send an email in HTML format.
6. Always offer a personal name if your postal system permits it; having a unique name in addition to your address helps to identify you more accurately.
7. Use a decent personal name.
8. Ensure that your message has a subject line at all times.
9. Give some thought to what the subject line will say.

About The Author

Dheeraj Mehrotra, MS, MPhil, PhD (Education Management) honoris causa., a white and a yellow belt in SIX SIGMA, a Certified NLP Business Diploma holder, is an Educational Innovator, Author, with expertise in Six Sigma In Education, Academic Audits, Neuro-Linguistic Programming (NLP), Total Quality Management In Education, an Experiential Educator, a CBSE Resource towards School Assessment (SQAA), CCE, JIT, Five S, and KAIZEN. He has authored over 100 books on topics which include Computer Science, AI, Digital Body Language, NLP, Quality Circles, School Management, Classroom Effectiveness and Safety and security in schools.

A former Principal at De Indian Public School, New Delhi, (INDIA), NPS International School, Guwahati, and Education Officer at GEMS, Gurgaon, with an ample teaching experience of over Two Decades, he is a certified Trainer for Quality Circles/ TQM in Education and QCI Standards for School Accreditation/ School Audits and Management. He has also been honoured with the President of India's National Teacher Award in the year 2006 and the Best Science Teacher State Award (By the Ministry of Science and Technology, State of UP), Innovation in Education for his inception of Six Sigma In Education by Education Watch, New Delhi and Education World- Best Teacher Award, BOLT Learner Teacher Award by Air India, 'Innovation in Education Award 2016' by Higher Education Forum (HEF), Gujarat Chapter, among others. He has developed over 150 FREE EDUCATIONAL MOBILE Apps for the Google Play Store exclusively for Teachers, Students, and Parents. This work has been

Books By The Same Author

9 798888 697733

Printed by Libri Plureos GmbH in Hamburg, Germany